Understanding
ISRAEL
Today

RAEL

Elisa Silverman

Mitchell Lane
PUBLISHERS
P.O. Box 196
Hockessin, Delaware 19707

A Kid's Guide to
THE MIDDLE EAST

Mitchell Lane
PUBLISHERS

Copyright © 2015 by Mitchell Lane Publishers, Inc. All rights reserved. No part of this book may be reproduced without written permission from the publisher. Printed and bound in the United States of America.

Printing   1   2   3   4   5   6   7   8   9

Library of Congress Cataloging-in-Publication Data
Silverman, Elisa.
  Understanding Israel today / by Elisa Silverman.
    pages cm. — (A kid's guide to the Middle East)
  Includes bibliographical references and index.
  ISBN 978-1-61228-650-1 (library bound)
  1. Israel—Juvenile literature. I. Title.
  DS102.95.S577 2014
  956.9405'4—dc23
                                                                2014021281
eBook ISBN: 9781612286730

PUBLISHER'S NOTE: This story is based on the author's extensive research, which she believes to be accurate. Documentation of such research is contained on pp. 59–61.

The Internet sites referenced herein were active as of the publication date. Due to the fleeting nature of some web sites, we cannot guarantee they will all be active when you are reading this book.

To reflect current usage, we have chosen to use the secular era designations BCE ("before the common era") and CE ("of the common era") instead of the traditional designations BC ("before Christ") and AD (*anno Domini,* "in the year of the Lord").

PBP

CONTENTS

BOLD words in text can be found in the glossary

The author has included pronunciations for many of the Hebrew words in this book. In these pronunciations, the letters "ch" are not pronounced like the "ch" in "children." Instead, the letters "ch" represent the Hebrew letter chet, which sounds like a "kh" or hard "h" sound, similar to the "ch" in "Loch Ness Monster."

Introduction

For such a tiny country, Israel tends to take up a lot of space in the world's imagination. Not many countries are reported on or discussed as often as Israel. Most of these reports and discussions focus on Israel and her neighbors. This makes some sense, since Israel's relations with others in the neighborhood are tense, important, and always in motion.

However, focusing only on Israel in relation to other countries hides another true face of Israel: the part that's just . . . Israel. Like any other country, there's an Israel that exists separate from international relations. Still, Israelis do take international issues very seriously. These issues have great impact on Israeli society. But Israel is more than just international challenges.

Israelis also have challenges and concerns about the direction of their country. They argue over government. They want a strong economy and community. They worry about social equality. Of course, some of Israel's **domestic** issues are international issues as well. The modern state of Israel was created within the land that was previously under British control called **Mandatory Palestine**. Many Arabs continue to live in the land that is now Israel, which has created problems at times. Today, the rest of the land that made up Mandatory Palestine is under Palestinian control. These areas, which border Israel, are Gaza

Jerusalem's Old City with a view of the Western Wall and the Dome of the Rock

and parts of the West Bank. There are frequent conflicts between Israelis and Palestinians in these regions.

Her People

Israel is the only country from the ancient world that was destroyed and then recreated in modern times. When the Jews were removed from ancient Israel, the **Diaspora** was created. Because of this, numerous Jewish ethnicities and cultures have developed over the last two thousand years. All those groups have started to come together again back in Israel.

Of course, while Israel is the world's only Jewish state, and the majority of her citizens are Jewish, there are other religions and cultures in Israeli society. In addition to the many subgroups of Jewish ethnicity within Israel, the country also has Arabs, Druze, Christians, Circassians, and Bedouin amongst its citizens. Each of these groups has its own interesting and unique identity within Israel.

Modern Israel is a fascinating little country with a rich and diverse local culture. Let's explore this nation together and find out what makes Israel—Israel.

A sister walks her younger brother to school in Jerusalem.

CHAPTER 1
Meet Ayelet

Ayelet is a busy eleven-year-old. But she's used to having a lot going on and she can handle it. She's the third-oldest in her family, which includes two sisters and three brothers. They all live with her *ima* (EE-mah) and *abba* (AH-bah) (mom and dad) in Neve (ne-VAY) Daniel, a town just south of Jerusalem.

Her day starts early. She has to be out to meet the school bus by seven in the morning. School gets out around two o'clock on most days, but at three one day a week. The school has a lot they want to teach! Ayelet's favorite subject is art. They paint a lot and do crafts. Her three favorite colors are blue, yellow, and pink. As she describes them, they're "elegant and quiet colors." She doesn't like the colors that are too bright or aggressive.

After school, Ayelet and her friends participate in many different activities. She's been taking ballet lessons since she was three years old. All the dance students put on a big performance each year. Once a week, Ayelet also takes lessons and does activities with Bnei Akiva (buh-NAY ah-KEY-vah). This is a religious **Zionist** youth group that's popular in Israel. Kids in this group learn life skills and Jewish values, enjoy scouting and hiking activities, and perform *chesed* (CHEH-sed)— community service.

When she's not in school or doing her activities, Ayelet spends a lot of time with her family. They really love to go on *tiyul* (tee-YOOL), which is Hebrew for "hike." Her favorite place to go on tiyul is up on the Golan, a mountainous region in Israel's northeast. "It's so beautiful and everything is so *poreach*

Ayelet, wearing a blue jacket, is with her brothers and sisters on a family hike on Givat Haturmusim (geev-AHT ha-toor-moo-SEEM), a popular hiking area south of Jerusalem.

(po-RAY-ach) and pretty," she explains. (Poreach means the flowers and trees are blooming.)

The Golan is a few hours' drive from Jerusalem, so she and her family also like to hike a lot closer to home. Ayelet says she and her siblings fight sometimes (well, all the time) if they're all sitting in the car too long. But she says the fights are just about stupid stuff, and they're all running around and happy as soon as they get out of the car and start hiking.

Golan, Israel

Ayelet is also planning a busy future for herself. She wants to be a mom to ten children, a ballet dancer, and prime minister of Israel. She wants to get married early enough to work on her different careers after raising her children.

Her role models are Golda Meir (may-EER), a former Israeli prime minister, and Rachel Imeinu (rah-CHEL ee-MAY-noo). She likes Golda because "she was prime minister and very *amitza* (ah-mee-TZAH) and she was a girl." (Amitza means courageous.) Rachel Imeinu, who is one of Judaism's biblical mothers, "was very organized and she took care of everything. And I think that's how I'm going to be. That's how I am," says Ayelet.

Golda Meir

Ayelet loves how pretty *Eretz Yisrael* (ER-itz yis-rah-EL)—the land of Israel—is, and how she can see history everywhere she goes. She thinks everyone should come for a visit to see it.

IN CASE YOU WERE WONDERING

What do Israeli kids like to eat?
Cottage cheese is a staple. It's a snack, or part of breakfast, lunch, or dinner. Ayelet really likes chicken and avocado burritos. But no cheese on these burritos. Ayelet and her family keep kosher. That means they only eat foods that are allowed under Jewish law. Meats (such as chicken) can't be eaten at the same meal as dairy foods (like cheese).

GOLDA MEIR

Golda Meir was the first woman to be prime minister of Israel and only the third woman in the world to ever earn that title. When she was a little girl in Kiev, Ukraine, she hardly could have imagined being prime minister, especially prime minister of a country that didn't exist yet!

She was born in Ukraine in 1898. Little Golda moved with her family to Wisconsin in 1906. She was married at just nineteen years old. Around this time, thousands of Jews were moving to British-controlled Mandatory Palestine. They often lived on community farms called *kibbutzim*. The members of a kibbutz worked together and provided for each other. Golda and her husband decided to move to Mandatory Palestine in 1921, where they lived on Kibbutz Merhavia.

Golda became involved in politics and played a large role in the creation of the State of Israel. She held many posts over the course of her career. She represented Israel as the nation's ambassador to the Soviet Union. She was a member of the Knesset (ki-NEH-set), the law-making branch of the Israeli government. She was also foreign minister, in charge of Israel's relationships with other countries.

Golda actually planned to retire before becoming prime minister. She was tired. She was also ill with leukemia, although people didn't know it at the time. When Israeli Prime Minister Levi Eshkol died in 1969, however, she was elected to take his place. She was now prime minister.

She resigned the post in 1974 after Israel suffered terribly during an attack by three Arab countries in the 1973 Yom Kippur War. Many Israelis were unhappy because they felt that the government was unprepared.

Throughout her political career, Golda was seen as strong, warm, and an effective and direct speaker. Israelis simply called her "Golda." With her grey bun and orthopedic shoes, Israelis viewed her as the country's grandmother.

This grandmother was also one of Israel's founding "fathers." She was one of only two women to sign Israel's declaration of independence in 1948. Golda said, "After I signed, I cried. When I studied American history as a schoolgirl and I read about those who signed the Declaration of Independence, I couldn't imagine these were real people. . . . And there I was sitting down and signing a declaration of independence."[1]

Golda died from her illness in Jerusalem in 1978.

Statue of King David with his famous harp, located in Jerusalem at the spot where the ancient king is believed to be buried.

CHAPTER 2
A Walk Down Memory Lane

There's a lot of history from the earliest days of ancient Israel to the modern state—here's the story in a nutshell.

The Ancient World

There's not much evidence to tell us exactly where the people called the "Israelites" came from. What's known is that this collection of separate yet related desert tribes lived on the land near the southeast corner of the Mediterranean Sea around three thousand years ago. As outside groups threatened the Israelites, the various tribes came together to defend themselves. Their first king was King Saul. This was the beginning of the period known as the United Monarchy around 1020 BCE. The Kingdom of Israel was born.

Israel's second king, King David, made Jerusalem the capital. His son King Solomon confirmed it as the religious center of the nation when he built the **Holy Temple** there. After King Solomon's death—around 930 to 920 BCE—the kingdom split into two. The southern kingdom was called "Judah," and the northern kingdom was called "Israel" or "Samaria."

At this time, the Assyrians, Babylonians, Egyptians, and other groups were fighting for control over the land in the Middle East. The Jewish kingdoms caught in the cross fighting didn't fare well. Israel was lost to the Assyrians around 720 BCE. Judah held on for another 134 years before the Babylonians conquered it and destroyed the Holy Temple in 586 BCE. By this time, Babylonia had already defeated the Assyrians and controlled the former Kingdom of Israel. Babylonia **exiled** most of the Jews from their land. With that, over four hundred years of Jewish nationhood in the land of Israel ended.

Soon, however, Persia defeated Babylonia and allowed the Jews to return to their homeland. They rebuilt their temple in Jerusalem, which was completed in 516 BCE. For the next four hundred years, Jews in the land of Israel were ruled by various foreign powers. Some of these powers allowed the Jews more freedoms than others.

Rome conquered the area in 63 BCE. Roman customs often conflicted with Jewish beliefs or freedoms. As more of these customs were brought to the Jewish province and Roman abuses of Jews became more common, the Jews began **revolting**. The Romans conquered Jerusalem and destroyed the second Holy Temple in 70 CE, but the revolts continued. By around 135 CE the Romans had had enough. They killed, exiled, or sold into slavery most of the Jews who were still living in the area. The Romans also eliminated the local area names of Judea (the Roman form of "Judah") and Samaria. They renamed this province "Palaestina" and Jerusalem was now called "Aelia Capitolina."

Muslims, Christians, and Jews in Israel

Jewish communities were now established in many places, including Europe, North Africa, and the Middle East. But by the seventh century, a new religion was forming in the Arabian Peninsula. Called Islam, the religion spread across the peninsula rapidly. Followers of Islam believed in only one god just as Jews and Christians did. Islam also taught that there had been many **prophets**, including Moses, Abraham, and Jesus. Muslims, as its followers were called, believed that Islam's most important figure, Muhammad, was the final prophet and that his teachings came directly from Allah (God). During the seventh and eighth

menorah

The Arch of Titus, constructed in 81 CE, still stands in Rome. It shows the Romans carrying the spoils of their victory in Jerusalem, including the destroyed Holy Temple's menorah.

centuries, Arab armies spread their new religion, their Arabic language, and their empire across the rest of the Middle East and beyond. The lands they conquered stretched from North Africa in the west to parts of China and India in the east. Like the Persians before them, the Arab rulers allowed Jews to return to Jerusalem and worship there.

Jews weren't the only ones who considered Jerusalem holy, though. Both Christianity and Islam have sacred sites located in the city. In 1095, Pope Urban II decided to fight the ruling Muslims so that Christians could visit these places. The wars that followed were called the Crusades, and they went on for almost two hundred years. While each group had its victories and losses over the course of the Crusades, Jews in the area suffered massacres under both groups. Even so, small groups of Jews began to move back to Jerusalem in the thirteenth century, coming from both Christian and Muslim lands.

As the Crusades were ending, another Muslim power in the region was growing stronger. The Turks were on the move. By the fifteenth century, they had conquered enough land to be considered an empire in their own right. Called the Ottoman Empire, it controlled most of the Middle East by the sixteenth century. Even though they were not Arab, the Turkish rulers shared the Islamic faith with much of the population under their control.

With a stable power in place, Jews from other lands again started to return to the land of Israel. They set up centers of Jewish study in Jerusalem and Safed.

Zionism and Modern Israel

While the Jews in the Middle East were living under Turkish rule, the Jews in Europe had a different experience. The ideas of nationalism and individual rights spread throughout Europe during the eighteenth and nineteenth centuries. Europeans began to see themselves as citizens of nations, not just members

IN CASE YOU WERE WONDERING

Where did the name "Zion" come from?
"Zion" is often used as a synonym for "Israel" or "Jerusalem." The word originated in the Jewish Bible. Over the years, the term became associated with not only the ancient holy land, but also the strong desire of Jews to return to it. One of the earliest and best-known uses of Zion in this way is found in Psalm 137: "By the rivers of Babylon—there we sat and also wept when we remembered Zion." Zion has appeared in prayers, poems, and other Jewish writings, symbolizing the longing of Jews to live in their historic homeland.

of smaller groups. This new way of thinking influenced a Hungarian-born Jew named Theodor Herzl. He is considered the father of political Zionism—the belief that Jews should live in an independent state in their historic homeland.

Herzl was convinced that European **anti-Semitism** would never allow Jews to be truly free in Europe. In 1895, he wrote a book called *The Jewish State*, which argued that Jews should leave Europe, ideally to live in Israel. Even before his book was published, thousands of Jews from Central and Eastern Europe had migrated to Israel. The migration increased with Zionism's spread. As Israel's Jewish population grew, the Arab population became increasingly resentful.

At the end of the First World War, the Ottoman Empire was broken up. European nations had temporary control of much of the Middle East. In 1922 the League of Nations formally gave the British Empire the mandate to administer the Palestine region. The British committed to the creation of a "national home for the Jewish people" in Palestine, without violating the civil rights of non-Jews living there.[1] Arabs and Jews would live together in this land, and the British would continue to govern Mandatory Palestine until the area could govern itself.

Meanwhile, in 1920, the Nazi Party was born in Germany. Adolf Hitler rose to power in this party and began to pass and enforce anti-Semitic laws. Jews moved to Mandatory Palestine in greater numbers in response. As the world moved toward war again, the British restricted Jewish immigration to Mandatory Palestine. Still, the threat of Nazism pushed Jews to continue to immigrate despite Britain's attempts to prevent it. At the end of the Second World War, the United Nations formally ended the British Mandate of Palestine. It proposed a new plan that partitioned the land of Mandatory Palestine into an Arab state and a Jewish state.

Jewish representatives accepted the UN partition plan, but the Arab leaders did not. Israel's first prime minister, David Ben-Gurion, issued Israel's declaration of independence on May 14, 1948, as the British Mandate expired.

The State of Israel

The day after independence was declared, multiple Arab armies invaded Israel. Israel's War of Independence ended in 1949. Since then, Israel has been in a hot and cold state of war with most of her neighbors. Arab countries founded the Palestinian Liberation Organization (PLO) in 1964 to fight for and establish an Arab state on the land instead of Israel.

Israel gained control of more land from Egypt, Syria, and Jordan during the Six Day War in 1967. Israel **annexed** some of the land it had captured, returned some of the land, and the status of some of the land is still disputed.

During this time, Israel has been the Middle East's lone stable democracy. It has also built a strong economy and vibrant culture atop the past three thousand years of Jewish history.

THE HOPE

"*HaTikvah*" (ha-TEEK-vah) is Israel's national anthem. In English, it translates to "The Hope." Like the American national anthem, "HaTikvah" is actually just the first part of a longer poem. Its lyrics describe the hope of Jews to return to their homeland. The original poem was written by Naphtali Herz Imber in 1878. He called it "*Tikvahtenu*" (teek-vah-TAY-noo), which is Hebrew for "Our Hope."

The poem was set to music by Samuel Cohen. While "HaTikvah" has been sung as Israel's national anthem since the founding of the modern state, it wasn't legally declared so by the Knesset until November 2004.

There are many English translations of "HaTikvah." Here's one:

As long as in the heart within,
The Jewish soul still yearns,
And toward the eastern edges onward,
An eye still gazes toward Zion.
Our hope is not yet lost,
The hope that is two thousand years old,
To be a free nation in our land,
The Land of Zion, Jerusalem.

The Hope is a statue that was sculpted by Naphtali Imber's grand-nephew, Nicky. Located in the northern town of Karmiel, it symbolizes the rebirth of the Jewish people in their land.

A Mizrachi Jew, originally from Yemen, is pictured here in Jerusalem in the early twentieth century.

CHAPTER 3
Jews in Israel

By the start of 2014, Israel's population had crossed the eight million mark.[1] Three-quarters of her population are Jewish; Arabs make up another 21 percent.[2] The rest of Israelis are non-Arab Christians, people of other religions, and those who have no religion.

Ashkenazim, Sephardim, and Mizrachim

When the Jews were expelled from ancient Israel by the Romans, the Jewish Diaspora was created. Spending the next two thousand years in countries all over the world led to the development of different Jewish ethnicities, each with their own traditions. Israel now has representatives from all these different communities.

There are three main Jewish ethnicities. The Ashkenazim (ahsh-kuh-NAH-zeem) are generally from Central and Eastern Europe. The Sephardim (suh-FAHR-deem) are descended from the Jews expelled from Spain and Portugal during the **Spanish Inquisition** in 1492. The third group, the Mizrachim (miz-RAH-cheem), are the Jews from North Africa, and those who never left the land of Israel or other areas of the Middle East.

After the Sephardim were forced out of Spain and Portugal, most of them moved to Mizrachi communities in the Middle East and North Africa. Because of this, both groups have developed many of the same traditions. People today often use "Sephardim" to refer to both Sephardim and Mizrachim. Israel's Jewish population is fairly evenly divided between Ashkenazim and Sephardim.

The great waves of Jewish immigration to Israel starting in the nineteenth century were mostly Ashkenazim. But as the modern State of Israel was established, leaders in Arab countries began making threats against the safety of the Jewish communities living there. A large number of the Sephardim living in these countries fled to Israel to escape this danger. Others were expelled in the years after Israel won its War of Independence. At this time, the Ashkenazim were well established in Israel, but the Sephardim had arrived with little to nothing. For a long time, Israeli Ashkenazim were more likely to study in universities, and usually earned more money than Israeli Sephardim. However, in recent years that gap has been closing.

All three of these groups follow **rabbinic Judaism**. So the religious laws and prayers of each group are quite similar, based on the same sacred texts and other documents. The Ashkenazi and Sephardi prayer books are a bit different, but religious Jews from either group would find the other familiar. However, there are distinct traditions and interpretations.

The holiday of Passover celebrates the Jews' freedom from slavery in Egypt over three thousand years ago. All Jews avoid eating **leavened** bread during this week-long holiday. But only Ashkenazim won't eat certain grains and beans during Passover. Ethiopian Jews (see page 27) are the only Jews who won't eat fermented dairy products like yogurt, butter, or cheese during the holiday.

Jewish holiday foods have much in common. At Passover, Jews traditionally hold a dinner called a seder. They eat foods like an unleavened bread called matzah, bitter herbs, and a fruit and nut paste called *charoset* (chah-ROW-set). Since Jews living around the world had different ingredients available to them, the exact recipes vary. For example, an Ashkenazi charoset will be made with apples, while a Sephardi charoset will have dates and figs.

A Seder plate

Some Jewish subgroups have also developed other holidays. Moroccan Jews have a holiday called *Mimouna* (mih-MOO-nah) which celebrates the end of Passover. After a week without leavened bread, Mimouna is marked by eating *mufleta* (moof-LEH-tah), a thin pancake covered in honey. The mufleta symbolizes the sweetness of freedom. While Mimouna is a Moroccan Jewish holiday, it's a tradition that more Israeli Jews, regardless of their ethnicity, are starting to celebrate as well.

Immigrants from the Former Soviet Union

Russian-speaking Jews are a distinct part of Israel's population. Most of these Jews are Ashkenazi, but some are Sephardi. After the Soviet Union broke up in 1991, nearly one million people from Russia, Ukraine, Belarus, and other former Soviet republics immigrated to Israel.[3] In a country Israel's size, that means nearly 15 percent of the population speaks Russian.[4] This is why if you call the electric company in Israel today, the recorded greeting will say: "Press one for Hebrew; two for Arabic; or three for Russian."

What's the favorite holiday of Israeli Jewish kids?
Definitely Purim. Everyone gets to dress up in crazy costumes, eat candy, and have parties. Purim celebrates the time when Haman, an advisor to the Persian king, wanted to kill all the Jews in the kingdom. Fortunately, the Jews stopped him.

One of the best treats from Purim are oznei haman (ohs-NAY ha-MAN) —yummy cookies with different fillings (see recipe on page 54). Oznei haman means "Haman's ears" in Hebrew.

The Soviet Union was officially an **atheist** state. Its laws made it difficult or impossible for people to practice any religion. Because of this, many of the Jews from the former Soviet Union aren't religious today. Indeed, many brought Christian spouses and family members with them. Before this group arrived, pork was not a common food in Israel, since neither Jews nor Muslims are allowed to eat it. Now, some Israeli supermarkets carry this meat, most likely if they're in a neighborhood with a large Soviet immigrant population.

Ethiopian Jews

For thousands of years, a community of Jews lived in Ethiopia. They were completely isolated from other Jews until the nineteenth century. The exact origins of the Ethiopian Jews are unclear, but according to their national tradition, they are the descendants of King Solomon and the Queen of Sheba.

Starting in the mid-1980s, the Israeli government began flying large groups of Jews out of Ethiopia and into Israel. They had suffered horribly in Ethiopia from anti-Semitism. They were even arrested and tortured for trying to leave. Over the next few decades, around ninety thousand Jews were brought to Israel from Ethiopia.[5] While individual Ethiopians have achieved success in Israel, including serving in the Knesset or becoming "Miss Israel," the community remains one of Israel's poorest.

Because Ethiopian Jews were cut off from the rest of world Jewry, their religious practice advanced differently. Their practices are based entirely in the Torah, the first five books of the Jewish Bible. As time went on, Jewish **rabbis** in the rest of the world interpreted the words of the Torah in different ways. They recorded their discussions and opinions in new religious works, like the Talmud. These writings contain many of the laws and customs observed by the majority of Jews today. The Jews in

Ethiopia, however, had never heard these teachings. As a result, Ethiopian Jews don't have rabbis. They are led by their *kessim* (keh-SEEM), which means "priests" or "elders." The kessim currently have no religious authority in Israel unless they study these additional Jewish laws and become rabbis. This is significant for the Ethiopian Jews, because it means that weddings performed by the kessim are not recognized by Israel.

One Ethiopian Jewish holiday that hasn't been a part of mainstream Judaism is *Sig'd*. On this day in the fall, Jews fast and repent for their sins. While still in Ethiopia, the Jews used the day to pray for a return to Jerusalem. Now that they're in Israel, they travel to Jerusalem to celebrate and pray for the coming of the Messiah.

Sig'd is slowly expanding beyond the Ethiopian community. As the holiday becomes more widely known in Israel, it's also become a time of celebrating Ethiopian Jewish culture.

Religious Subgroups

Jews in Israel are not just different because of their ethnicities. Some Jews are very strict in following all of the Jewish laws and practices, while others follow very few, or even none. The *Haredim* (ha-rey-DEEM), or ultra-Orthodox, are made up of many distinct subgroups. Each of these groups practices a very strict form of Judaism according to their interpretations of the laws. The Zionist *Dati Leumi* (dah-TEE lay-oo-MEE), or "national religious," are also Orthodox Jews, but their interpretations of Jewish laws often differ from the Haredim.

Beyond this, most inter-Jewish designations in Israel are less formal. People describe themselves using a variety terms, such as traditional, religious, or some combination. These terms also mean different things to different people. On Shabbat, a strict religious family will light candles before sunset on Friday,

A group of ultra-Orthodox Jewish students on their way to yeshiva, where they study Torah and other religious texts. They are careful to never trim their sidelocks.

attend **synagogue**, and avoid doing any prohibited activities until the day is over, such as working, driving, writing, or using electricity. However, another family may describe itself as "traditional" because they keep Shabbat as a family day, driving out to spend the day at the beach together instead.

Nearly half of Israel's Jews describe themselves as **secular**.[6] Even so, most secular Israeli Jews participate in some Jewish religious practices at some time, such as lighting Shabbat candles, keeping kosher, or going to synagogue.[7] Regardless of how an Israeli Jew describes their religious observance, the vast majority go to synagogue at least sometimes and participate in a Passover seder each year.[8]

Bar Mitzvah ceremony at the Western Wall in Jerusalem's Old City.

IN CASE YOU WERE WONDERING

What's a Bar or Bat Mitzvah all about anyway?
Mitzvah (meetz-VAH) means "commandment" in Hebrew. *Bar* and *bat* mean "son" and "daughter." At the age of twelve or thirteen, a young Jew becomes a daughter or son of the commandments, regardless of whether there's a big party. That means they have new responsibilities and rights as a full member of the Jewish community. It's becoming increasingly popular for Jews from all over the world to have their children's bar or bat mitzvah celebrations in Israel to emphasize the religious aspect of the event.

THE SAMARITANS

Samaritans are a tiny Jewish sect in Israel. While there were once hundreds of thousands of Samaritans, only around eight hundred remain today. They live in Holon, outside Tel Aviv, and in a village called Kiryat Luza, atop Mount Gerizim.

The ancestors of the Samaritans lived in the northern Kingdom of Israel. They broke with mainstream Judaism over two thousand years ago. Their holiest site is Mount Gerizim, not Jerusalem. They don't recognize rabbinic Judaism, or any religious texts other than the Torah.

Samaritans call themselves *B'nai Yisrael* (bu-NAY yis-rah-EL), the Children of Israel, and *Shamerim* (shah-meh-REEM), the Observant Ones. They often have both Hebrew and Arabic names. They also still organize themselves in a very traditional way, turning to elders who make decisions for the entire community.

Samaritans during their annual pilgrimage to the top of Mount Gerizim for Passover. Unique among other Jewish communities, only the Samaritans continue to perform an ancient animal sacrifice ritual during the Passover pilgrimage. The sacrificed sheep are then roasted and served with matzah and bitter herbs.

Two friends from the Israel Defense Forces taking a break. Israel is one of only a few countries in the world that requires women to serve in the military. Women have taken part in Israel's military since before the founding of the state in 1948.

CHAPTER 4
Israel's Muslims, Christians, and Druze

While non-Jewish Israelis make up only a quarter of the population, they also come from a variety of different ethnicities and traditions.

Muslim Arabs

The majority of Israeli Arabs are Muslim and the majority of Israeli Muslims are Arab—but not all.

Following the death of Muhammad, Muslims broke into two groups. The Sunnis believed that the next Muslim leader should be elected by the community. The Shiites believed that only Muhammad's relatives should be allowed to lead. The groups developed slightly different practices over time. Today, most Muslims around the world are Sunni, and the same is true in Israel. They live primarily in villages in northern Israel. Israeli Arabs are Israeli citizens, unlike Palestinian Arabs, who live in disputed territories. One of the growing issues in Israeli society is the degree to which Israeli Arabs identify with the Palestinians, or *as* Palestinians, instead of as Israelis. Israeli Arabs are not required to serve in Israel's military, the Israel Defense Forces (IDF), like Israeli Jews are.

Israeli Arabs participate in Israeli government. They have political parties and members of Knesset who represent them. Village governments are all elected locally, so the many mayors and council representatives in their communities are Arab as well. However, Arab communities have historically received less funding for public services and education than Jewish communities. The Israeli government has been working to change this approach. It hopes to provide equal services to all citizens so Arabs will feel that they are a valued part of Israeli society, too.

When the state of Israel was formed, Jerusalem was divided in two—only West Jerusalem was under Israeli control; the eastern portion was under Jordanian control. Today, both Israelis and Palestinians consider the area their own, but it is governed by Israel. The Arabs who live in East Jerusalem are in a unique position. They can apply for Israeli citizenship. These residents have traditionally protested against Israel by not taking Israeli citizenship. However, applications for Israeli citizenship from East Jerusalem Arabs have been increasing since 2008. Many believe that this is because they want to protect their rights as inhabitants of the city.

Bedouin

The Bedouin (beh-doe-WIN) are Arab and Muslim, but they are a culturally distinct community. Most Bedouin live in the Negev Desert in southern Israel. A smaller community of them live up north in the Galil.

Traditionally, they're **nomadic** tribes, but that lifestyle has all but vanished since the 1990s. Unfortunately, their nomadic

IN CASE YOU WERE WONDERING

Do Jewish and Arab kids in Israel ever hang out together?
It's hard to put a number on how or when they might just "hang out." However, there are a number of organizations that work to bring Jewish and Arab kids together. Most schools only serve their community, which makes them generally Jewish religious, Jewish secular, or Arab schools. Some new kinds of schools are opening in Israel that bring together a mixed Arab and Jewish student body and curriculum.

There have also been a number of youth music groups and orchestras made up of Jewish and Arab teens. These programs are designed to bring the groups together, and increase trust and social bonds between them.

past has made it difficult for the Israeli government to determine who owns the land they lived in. Even though the Bedouin have settled into villages in the Negev, many of those villages aren't recognized as official towns. These unrecognized villages don't receive public services, such as electricity or water, which makes life there very difficult.

Israelis have different ideas about how to solve this problem. The government recently proposed a plan to give some of the unrecognized towns official status. Not everyone likes this plan, however. That's because only some towns would be recognized with official status. Many others would be torn down, and the Bedouin who live there would have to move.

Many people think it is unfair to move a local population off their land. The government leaders who developed the plan say that the government can't afford to provide services to every Bedouin village, as many are in remote desert areas. They believe that their plan is the best way to get the Bedouin living in modern communities.

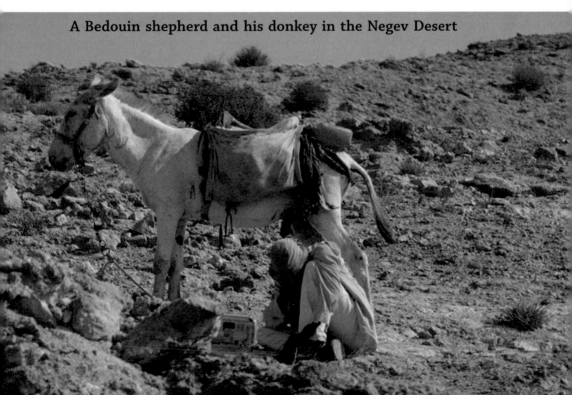

A Bedouin shepherd and his donkey in the Negev Desert

Even with the challenges facing them today, the Bedouin do generally identify as Israeli. They're not required to do so, but many of them have served in the IDF since Israel was founded. Bedouins commonly serve in tracking units, which protect Israel's northern and southern borders. Trackers look for evidence of illegal border crossings and find the intruders before they can cause harm to Israelis. Bedouin trackers say that their connection to the land is their best tool in keeping it safe.

Circassians

The Circassians (sur-CASH-ins) are another Sunni Muslim community, but they aren't Arab. Unlike the Bedouin, all of their men are required to serve in the IDF by law. This community is originally from the Caucasus region, located at the border between Europe and Asia. In a nineteenth-century war, the Russians conquered their homeland, leaving them homeless. They relocated to the Ottoman Empire, including the land that is now part of Israel.

Sochi, now in Russia, is their historical capital. Some Circassians dream of reclaiming their capital and land, while others believe their lives are now in Israel. In either case, their common experience of expulsion from their land has created a bond between them and Israeli Jews.

There are roughly three thousand Circassians living in northern Israel today. It's a close community and they don't often marry outsiders. They speak Circassian among themselves, which has helped preserve their culture in Israel.

Christians

There are Arab and non-Arab Christian citizens in Israel, but most are Arab. They represent a full spectrum of Christianity, including Greek Catholic, Greek Orthodox, Armenian, and Coptic.

Israeli Circassians in traditional dress, carrying their traditional calvary swords and the Circassian flag.

Most Israeli Christians live in northern Israel. They tend to have fewer children and lower unemployment rates than Israeli Muslims do. Israeli Christians also do better in school than Israeli Jews, on average.

One of the most significant Christian celebrations in Israel is the Easter Holy Fire ceremony. This celebration takes place on the day before Easter Sunday. Christians fill the Church of the Holy Sepulchre, which is said to be built on the place where Jesus was buried in Jerusalem. In the church and its courtyard, worshipers hold unlit candles. All the lights go off and everyone is silent. At two o'clock in the afternoon, it is believed that a sunbeam enters the church and lights a lamp which is in Jesus's tomb. The head bishop of the Greek Orthodox Church of Jerusalem uses this lamp to light other candles, which are in turn used to pass the flame around. The church quickly fills with light as this Holy Fire spreads from person to person.

Like other Arabs, Christian Arabs aren't drafted into the IDF. Some do volunteer. The numbers of Christian Arabs choosing to serve in the IDF has always been quite low, but these numbers have been increasing of late. In 2014, government leaders suggested that the IDF begin drafting Christian Arabs. At least one Christian Arab Knesset member opposes this, saying that it is an attempt by Israel to create division between Muslim and Christian Arabs.[1]

The Choir of the Canons is one of the main areas within the Church of the Holy Sepulchre, dating from the time of the Crusades. The two thrones at either side of the room are for the Greek Orthodox Patriarchs of Jerusalem and Antioch.

While the uptick in Arab Christians volunteering for the IDF represents only a small number, it is part of a wider movement within the community to distinguish Itself as a distinct Israeli group. This movement has not been accepted by all Arab Christians in Israel, but it is growing. Israeli Christians formed a political party in 2013, and some members are calling for Christian history to be taught in Arab schools in addition to Arab-Muslim history.

Druze

The Druze are a particularly interesting community, even though they make up only about 2 percent of the Israeli population. They speak Arabic and are generally considered to be part of the Israeli Arab community. They live in northern Israel.

We don't know much about the Druze religion. They're very secretive about their religious practices. It is known that they believe in one god. One of their main religious values is a sense of brotherliness and community. They don't accept converts. One is either born Druze or one isn't.

As a result, Druze communities work together to help young people find a spouse. Druze in Israel and Syria have

---

IN CASE YOU WERE WONDERING

Who takes care of the non-Jewish holy sites in Israel?
Holy sites are the responsibility of their respective religious authorities. The Church of the Holy Sepulchre is run by a very complicated web of different Christian authorities, each representing a different **denomination**. Some Christian groups have responsibility for repairing specific shrines or areas of the church, which can make things confusing, but they work it out. The Al-Aqsa **Mosque** in Jerusalem is Islam's third holiest site. Muslims believe that Muhammad traveled to this mosque from Mecca in a single night to begin his most important spiritual journey. The mosque is run by the Jerusalem Islamic Waqf. In all instances, Israel is responsible for keeping the locations secure and safe.

moved to each other's countries for marriage. This is very hard for them as they can't go back to visit their family members who remain in their original country. Part of Druze culture is to be loyal to the state where they live. This is the reason that there are so many Druze men in the IDF.

The town of Isfiya in northern Israel was established in the seventeenth century by Druze migrating from Lebanon. The town hosts an annual festival of Druze culture. Indeed the town, known for its warm hospitality, welcomes visitors all year around to experience local foods, crafts, and arts.

CROSSING THE NORTHERN BORDER

The Shouting Hill is in the Golan about 1.5 miles from Israel's border with Syria. There are no direct relations between Israel and Syria. So before Skype and Facebook, Druze would go up to the hill with binoculars and megaphones to get the news from family and friends living in Syria.

More recently, Israel set up a field hospital along her border with Syria. There, IDF medical personnel treated Syrians wounded in that country's civil war. Hospitals in Israel's northern areas have also been treating adults and children with serious injuries. For better or worse, Israel's northern hospitals have a lot of experience treating the physical and mental traumas of war. They now use that experience to care for these unusual patients.

Israeli medical staff, both Jewish and Arab, attend to the Syrians. The Syrian patients are often nervous and suspicious at first. In addition to being hurt in the Syrian civil war, they now find themselves in a country they've been taught to hate. However, with time and care, that perspective starts to change. Fourteen-year-old Ahmed was fitted for prosthetics in Israel after losing his legs in a bomb blast in Syria. According to him, "They said Israelis are our enemy, but they're nice."[2]

View into Syria from the Golan

On May 14, 1948, David Ben-Gurion gave a speech declaring the creation of the State of Israel. Hanging on the wall is a photo of Theodor Herzl, who was a key founder of the modern Zionist movement to build a Jewish State.

CHAPTER 5
Six Million Prime Ministers

Israel is not an easy country to govern. Golda Meir is reported to have described the situation to former US President Richard Nixon during one of their meetings in the 1970s. "You are the president of 150 million Americans; I am the prime minister of 6 million prime ministers," she explained.[1]

Israelis may all think they know how to govern better than the actual prime minister, but Israel does have just one. Israel is a parliamentary democracy. That means that the executive branch, which is responsible for the operation of the country, answers to the legislative branch, which makes the laws. The judicial branch, which interprets the laws, is separate. The prime minister and cabinet members make up the executive branch, while the legislative branch in Israel is called the Knesset.

The Knesset has 120 members. Israel's first prime minister, David Ben-Gurion, thought this was too many for such a small country.[2] However, many Israelis appreciated the symbolism of the number. The *Knesset Hagedolah* (the "Great Assembly"), which met as the Jewish council in Jerusalem starting in the sixth century BCE, also had 120 members.

Elections
National elections for the Knesset must be held at least every four years. The Knesset can call for early elections, however. This can be done by the prime minister if he or she is feeling politically strong. It can also be done by the opposition who believe they have a majority and can take over the government.

Israel has a large number of political parties, many of which come and go. Two of the largest and oldest political parties are Likud and Labor. The Likud has its origins in a stream of Zionism focused on a strong military and free market economy. The Labor party has its origins in **socialism**, and historical ties to the country's unions and working the land. Recently, a number of new political parties have formed, placing themselves between these two sides.

Israel also has many smaller parties that represent a single group of people. There are some parties that represent ultra-Orthodox Jews, for example. Other parties represent the Arab citizens of Israel.

Political parties are important in Israel's elections because Israeli citizens don't vote for people. They vote for a political party. The percentage of votes a party receives determines how many seats they will hold in the Knesset. With the support of a majority of the other members of the Knesset, one Knesset member is chosen to become prime minister.

In the next election, political parties will have to get at least 3.25 percent of the national vote in order to be represented in the Knesset. As late as the 2013 elections, a political party only

The Knesset building, completed in 1966. The Israeli government held a public competition calling for building designs to house Israel's parliament. The competition was won by architect Joseph Klarwein. His design was noted for its simplicity and unity.

IN CASE YOU WERE WONDERING

Does Jewish law apply to everyone?

No. Israel refers to itself as a "Jewish and democratic state,"[3] and protects the religious freedoms of all its citizens. It is a secular state, meaning that its laws are not based on any religion. However, there are definitely areas where religion, law, and public life mix. For example, government offices are closed on Jewish holidays and the Jewish sabbath.

Some family law is governed by religious authorities, but all religious groups refer to their own authorities. **Civil marriage** doesn't exist under Israeli law. Instead, Jews, Muslims, and Christians who wish to marry or divorce must turn to their respective religious leaders.

needed to capture 2 percent of the national vote. The smaller political parties, which generally represent specific groups of people or a single political issue like environmentalism, don't like this change. They say it will cut them out of the Knesset.

However, many other Israelis feel these smaller parties have too much power. They can be the deciding factor when forming a new government, and a coalition needs just two or three more Knesset votes. They may agree to join only if other members of Knesset support their causes in exchange.

The law is expected to encourage multiple small parties that represent the same group or interest to work together. Separately, the small parties may not reach 3.25 percent, but together they could.

Other Big Israeli Issues

The electoral threshold law isn't the only issue on Israelis' minds. Here are other issues that have Israelis talking:

Conscription of Ultra-Orthodox Jews

There is a mandatory draft into the Israel Defense Forces that applies to most Israelis, certainly to most Israeli Jews. However, a large number of draft exemptions are given to ultra-Orthodox Jews, as long as they remain studying in a Jewish religious school called a yeshiva. Instead of serving in the IDF along with other secular and religious Jews, Haredi men usually choose to stay in yeshiva. Many of them believe they're serving the Jewish nation best by studying Torah and keeping Jewish traditions alive.

In a nation surrounded by enemies, a large military is essential to ensure the safety of all of Israel's citizens. Most Israeli men and women take on the risks associated with military service in order to protect their country. The fact that the Haredim enjoy this protection but don't have to share in the risks is not fair, some Israelis say. A bill limiting religious exemptions recently passed in the Knesset. It is strongly opposed by the Haredi community.

Cost of Living

In recent years, the cost of living has risen steeply for Israelis. The price of cottage cheese, an Israeli diet mainstay, jumped 40 percent in three years.[4] The cost of renting a home in Tel Aviv also jumped 40 percent in six years.[5] In 2011 there were widespread protests against a variety of social and economic issues. Different protesters had different priorities, but there were protests against rising prices, lack of business competition due to a few Israeli corporations holding a lot of economic power, and increasing gaps between the rich and the poor.

Not everyone can agree on a solution, however. Members of Knesset have formed committees to address these issues, but so far most Israelis are frustrated that there's been little change.

BENJAMIN NETANYAHU

Israel's current prime minister is Benjamin Netanyahu. He is also known as "Bibi," a boyhood nickname. Netanyahu represents the Likud party, which is known for its commitment to a strong defense for Israel.

Netanyahu has been prime minister since 2009. He was elected to the office once before in 1996, but lost the 1999 election. He left politics before returning in 2002 as Israel's foreign minister, and then becoming its finance minister.

Netanyahu grew up in Jerusalem, although as a teenager he lived in a suburb of Philadelphia. He returned to Israel in 1967 to join the IDF. He served in the Sayeret Matkal, a special forces unit that works to fight terrorism and rescue hostages. While a member, he participated in many dangerous missions abroad. His older brother Yonatan had also been a member of Sayeret Matkal. In 1976, Yoni was killed during one of its missions, a tragedy that affected Netanyahu deeply.

As of today, Netanyahu has the distinction of having been Israel's youngest prime minister. Aside from David Ben-Gurion, he's also now Israel's longest-serving prime minister.

Prime Minister Benjamin Netanyahu speaks at the official ceremony opening a new highway connecting Tel Aviv and Jerusalem, January 6, 2010.

Israel's "Iron Dome," its anti-missile defense system. Here the Iron Dome launches a rocket that will destroy a missile fired by Hamas into Israel. The Iron Dome's rocket destroys the missile in the air, before it can land in Israel. Israel reports that the Iron Dome has a 90 percent success rate in its attempts to destroy and prevent missiles from hitting populated areas of Israel.

CHAPTER 6
Israel and the World

Israel lives in a bit of a rough neighborhood. So international and security issues are a strong presence in the day-to-day lives of Israelis.

Palestinians
In 1993 and 1995, Israeli and Palestinian representatives signed the Oslo Accords, in hopes of achieving peace. Both Israelis and Palestinians had obligations under this agreement. Israel would begin to move forces out of designated Palestinian areas, paving the way for Palestinians to govern themselves in the West Bank and Gaza. Palestinians would recognize Israel's right to exist and stop using violence to achieve their goals. The Palestinian Authority (PA) was created as the governing entity in charge of Gaza and the West Bank. Both sides have violated the terms of the agreement since that time, however. As a result, the peace process has been starting and stopping for many years.

An organization called Hamas won a majority of parliamentary seats in the 2006 Palestinian Authority elections. This group calls for the destruction of Israel and is considered a terrorist organization by Israel, the United States, and many other nations. In 2007, Hamas took over Gaza entirely, effectively splitting the area's administration from the PA. This division with the PA and Hamas's continued violence against Israel have made the peace process even more complex.

According to Netanyahu, the Israeli people have "achieved a wide national **consensus** on the idea of two states for two peoples."[1] As for Israelis themselves, most don't think that peace will come any time soon. A majority want to have peace talks with the Palestinians, even though they don't really expect them to bring peace.[2]

Unfortunately, recent peace talks haven't included discussions of what are often called "final status" issues. These are issues that could finally resolve the conflict once and for all: agreeing on borders, deciding what will happen to Palestinians living outside Israel and the disputed territories, ending terrorism, and determining who will control East Jerusalem. Instead of addressing these issues, American, Israeli, and Palestinian representatives spend a lot of time going back and forth on whether:

- Israel can build more homes in Jewish towns located in the West Bank
- Israel should release Palestinians prisoners who've been convicted of terrorist acts
- the Palestinian Authority should seek international recognition as an independent state
- the Palestinian Authority should recognize Israel as a Jewish state

Israelis are divided on the issue of expanding Jewish housing in the West Bank, and whether some Jewish towns and settlements should be disbanded as part of a peace agreement. However, a majority of Israelis oppose the release of convicted Palestinian terrorists.[3] For Israelis whose family members died at the hands of the Palestinian prisoners, these releases are particularly emotionally painful. Another criticism is that it undermines the justice system to release people who've been convicted of crimes. Many also believe these releases only encourage Palestinian terrorists to kidnap more Israelis.

Some Palestinian groups, including Hamas, have kidnapped Israeli soldiers and citizens in the past and agreed to release them only if Palestinian prisoners were released from Israel. Hamas uses the threat of more kidnappings to instill fear in the Israeli public. In part to make kidnappings easier, the group built numerous underground tunnels that cross the border from Gaza into Israel. Hamas members wanted to abduct or kill Israelis and disappear back into the ground using these tunnel systems. The IDF destroyed many of these tunnels during a war fought between Gaza and Israel in 2014.

Negotiators hope that in time, the interim issues can be resolved and trust can be built between Israelis and Palestinians, which could eventually lead to a final peace agreement. Unfortunately, it isn't really working so far. Each side seems to hold the other with the same high level of distrust.[4]

Iran

Of all the threats Israel faces, Iran's program to develop **nuclear weapons** is often considered by Israelis to be one of the most serious. Iranian leaders' calls for Israel's complete destruction increase Israelis' concern. Most Israelis take Iran at its word and see the nation as a threat to Israel's existence, if it possesses nuclear weapons.[5] The United States, Britain, and other countries are negotiating with Iran to limit its nuclear weapons program. Many Israeli leaders believe that these countries are not taking Iran's threats seriously enough, however. As Iranian demands continue to grow, it's difficult to predict how strongly the United States and other countries will act to keep Iran from gaining the ability to develop nuclear weapons.

Comments by Israeli officials have caused many to wonder if Israel is closer to making a military strike against Iran. The attacks would target sites where nuclear weapons are thought to be in development. Not everyone is confident in this approach, however. Since other nations are negotiating with Iran, Israel would have to attack on its own. Israelis worry that a strike might not be able to destroy enough of the program to reduce the threat.

Israel isn't eager to take military action. However, according to Prime Minister Benjamin Netanyahu, Israel won't rule out an attack on Iran. "The more credible the threat of force on Iran," he said, "the smaller the chance that force will ever have to be used."[6]

A nuclear attack isn't the only threat that Iran poses to Israel. Iran provides support to Hezbollah in Lebanon and Hamas in Gaza, two groups that launch attacks against Israel. Israel has captured or prevented the delivery of large numbers of weapons on their way from Iran to Lebanon and Gaza for use against Israel. These attacks include firing rockets into Israeli towns near the borders, as well as **suicide bombings** in cities deeper inside Israel.

IN CASE YOU WERE WONDERING

What sports do Israelis compete in?

Two of Israel's most popular sports are soccer and basketball. Maccabi Electra Tel Aviv, one of Israel's professional basketball teams, won the Euroleague Basketball Championship for the sixth time in 2014. Israel's national soccer team has only qualified for the World Cup once, in 1970, but they continue to try.

Gal Fridman is the only Israeli to win an Olympic gold medal, which he won at the 2004 Games in Athens in sailing. Israelis have won other Olympic medals in sailing, as well as in judo and canoeing. Israeli athletes also compete in international tennis tournaments and ice skating competitions.

WHAT'S IN A NAME?

Occupied territory. Disputed territory. Judea and Samaria. The West Bank. A small plot of land with so many names. This kidney-shaped area of land located along the west bank of the Jordan River was captured by Israel from Jordan during the Six Day War in 1967. Palestinians, who are the majority in the area, want the land to become the foundation for the Palestinian state.

Many Jews refer to the area as Judea and Samaria. This is the Roman version of the name of the area dating back to ancient times when the land was part of the Jewish kingdoms. The more neutral names are disputed territory or the West Bank. These terms don't imply ownership, legal status, or right of either Israel or the Palestinians, but are simply descriptive.

Today, the West Bank is formally divided into three administrative zones. Area A is the territory under full control of the Palestinian Authority. Area B is territory over which the PA has full civil control, but Israel retains security control. Area C territory is under full Israeli control.

Regardless of what it's called, who the land belongs to is one of the main points of argument between Israel and the Palestinian Authority. Here is a prime example where international and domestic issues are one and the same for Israel.

The questions are many. How will the land be divided? Will it be divided? Can the Jewish communities there grow, and can new ones be added? Would the Jews currently living in the West Bank be allowed to stay if the land was governed by the PA? Would attacks by Palestinians end if a Palestinian state were created in the West Bank?

These questions and more are constantly being discussed as part of the vague ongoing discussion called "the peace process."

OZNEI HAMAN

There are two parts to making oznei haman, the cookie dough and the filling. This recipe makes 60 cookies. **Be sure to make these cookies with adult permission and supervision.**

Dough Ingredients

3 eggs
1 cup sugar
¾ cup oil
1/3 cup apple or orange juice
1 tablespoon vanilla extract
5–5½ cups flour
1 tablespoon baking powder

Poppy Seed Filling

1 can poppy seed filling
   (12½ ounces)
1 egg
½ cup sugar
3 tablespoons strawberry jam
1 cup raisins

Instructions

1. In a large bowl, mix together the eggs and sugar, beat until creamy. Add oil, juice, and vanilla and mix.
2. In a separate medium sized bowl, sift together the flour and baking powder. Slowly add the dry ingredients into the egg mixture, stirring as you go. Continue mixing until you have a smooth dough. Cover the bowl with plastic wrap and refrigerate for one hour.
3. While you wait for the dough to chill, make your poppy seed filling. Just blend all the ingredients together.
4. When the dough is ready, preheat the oven to 350°F. Roll the dough out so it is ⅛ to ¼ inch thick. Make sure it is thick enough to hold the filling without breaking!
5. The shape of the oznei haman is key. So be sure to fold the dough over the filling just right. Use a round 3-inch cookie cutter to cut out the cookies. You can also use the top of a cup or glass, but be sure it's at least 3 inches wide so there's enough room for the filling.
6. Put a teaspoon of filling in the center of one dough circle.
7. Fold over the top left side of the dough circle so it covers about ⅓ of the width of the filling.
8. Fold over the top right side of the dough an equal amount, so that the top left and top right folds form a point at the top of the circle.
9. Fold up the bottom part of the dough an equal amount to make two additional points with the other two folds. A triangle of filling should still be visible in the center.
10. Tuck the left end of the bottom fold under the left side fold. Each side should now have one side on top and the other side underneath another fold. This will help keep the filling from falling out as the cookies bake.
11. Repeat with the remaining cookies.
12. Place on lined or greased cookie sheets and bake for 10 to 12 minutes.

SUKKOT LANTERN

Sukkot is a seven-day holiday which commemorates the forty years that Jews spent in the desert without permanent homes after escaping slavery in Egypt. The festival also celebrates the harvest. Today, Jews in Israel and all over the world celebrate the holiday by eating and even sleeping outside in a shelter called a sukkah. The roof of the sukkah is often made with palm fronds or other tree branches, so that at night the stars can be seen through the roof. Families begin to build their sukkah several days (or sometimes weeks) before the holiday, and kids help by making decorations which are hung from the ceiling beams or on the walls.

Here's a decorative lantern that you can make with a soda bottle and tissue paper. **Be sure to make this craft with adult supervision!**

Materials
Newspaper or old cloth to protect
    your work area
Clear plastic soda bottle with
    labels removed
Scissors
Colored tissue paper
Disposable bowl
Glue
Water
Paint brush
Hole Punch
String or wire

Instructions
1. Cover your work area with newspaper or an old cloth.
2. Cut the top and bottom off of the soda bottle to create a cylindrical shape.
3. Decide on a design for your lantern, and cut tissue paper into strips, squares, or whatever other shapes you would like to use.
4. Put some glue in the disposable bowl, add a small amount of water (about half as much water as glue), and mix.
5. With the paint brush, "paint" the outside of the soda bottle with glue.
6. Apply your tissue paper to the bottle, and then paint the paper with more glue. Make sure that the paper gets completely wet.
7. Once the glue is completely dry, punch two holes on opposite sides of the top of your lantern.
8. Decide how low you would like your lantern to hang from the ceiling, and cut a piece of string about 2½ times as long. (For example, if you want to leave 1 foot between the ceiling and your lantern, cut your string about 2½ feet long.)
9. Tie the two ends of the string to the two holes you punched at the top of your lantern, and hang.
10. You can also try making lanterns with different patterns, colors, or bottle shapes!

WHAT YOU SHOULD KNOW ABOUT ISRAEL

Official name: State of Israel

Official languages: Hebrew and Arabic

- Hebrew was used only in prayer and Jewish study of the Bible for nearly two thousand years until the nineteenth century, when Eliezer Ben-Yehuda revived it as a daily language.
- Both languages are written from right to left, and often without using any vowels!

The Israeli Calendar:

- The work/school week runs from Sunday through Thursday, although many people also have some school or work on Friday mornings.
- Some years, Israel has thirteen months! Israel uses two calendars: the Gregorian calendar, like much of the Western world, and the Jewish calendar. The Jewish calendar is a lunisolar calendar, which means it's organized around both the sun and moon. So instead of having an extra day every four years, it has an entire extra month every so often!

Israel is a popular tourist destination for birds.

- Hundreds of millions of birds move along the thermal currents that flow from Central Africa through Israel's narrow stretch into Asia and Europe. The Hula Valley, in the Galil, is a main bird layover site on their journey.
- Around 540 different bird species come for a visit, including raptors and cranes. Fall is their favorite season to visit.

The lowest point on Earth is in Israel. The Dead Sea is 1,388 feet (423 meters) below sea level. Everything floats in the Dead Sea because of its high salt content at around 33 percent. In contrast, most oceans and seas have salt concentrations around 3 percent!

The Mount of Olives cemetery in Jerusalem has been in use for over three thousand years and remains a popular final resting place for Jews from all over the world.

Israel ranks the highest in the world for time spent on online social networks, averaging 11.1 hours per month.[1]

Israel is roughly the size of New Jersey in the United States.

FLAG: The flag of Israel consists of a white background with horizontal blue stripes at the top and the bottom. In the middle of the flag is a blue Star of David. The Star of David (Magen David) is also known as the Jewish star and is a symbol of Judaism. The white background with two blue stripes of the flag was modeled after the traditional Jewish prayer shawl.

TIMELINE

BCE

ca. 1020–1007 King Saul reigns as the first king of the United Monarchy in the ancient land of Israel.

ca. 1006–970 King David reigns as king of the Jewish nation and establishes Jerusalem as its capital.

ca. 930–920 King Solomon dies and the United Monarchy splits into two Jewish kingdoms: Judah in the south and Israel (or "Samaria") in the north.

720 The northern kingdom of Israel is lost to the Assyrians.

586 Babylonia, which had been conquering Assyrian territory for the past few decades, conquers Judah, sacks Jerusalem, destroys the Holy Temple, and exiles the Jews.

539 Persian emperor Cyrus the Great issues "The Decree of Return for the Jews," permitting Jews who'd been exiled from Israel to return.

63 Rome conquers the area and makes it the Judea province of its empire.

CE

70 After multiple Jewish revolts to Roman rule, the Romans take control of Jerusalem and destroy the Second Holy Temple.

135 Romans expel Jews from Judea and Samaria and give the area a new name, "Palaestina."

635–638 The land located in modern-day Israel falls to the Muslim Conquest; Jews are permitted to return to Jerusalem under Muslim rule.

1211 A group of rabbis and Jewish scholars from France and England return to Israel, sparking a few hundred years of increased Jewish migration back to Israel.

ca. 1500 The Ottoman Empire becomes the dominant force throughout the Middle East, North Africa, and parts of Europe.

1860 Mishkenot Sha'ananim, the first Jewish neighborhood outside the walls of the Old City in Jerusalem, is established.

1882 The first wave of significant Jewish immigration from Russia and Eastern Europe to Israel (called the First Aliyah) begins.

1909 Tel Aviv is founded.

1917 Balfour Declaration is issued by the British government, declaring support for a "national home for the Jewish people" in Palestine.

1947 The United Nations proposes the Partition Plan for Palestine that would split the remaining land in the Palestine region into one Jewish and one Arab state; the plan is accepted by Jewish representatives, but rejected by the Arabs.

1948 The British Mandate over Palestine ends and the Jewish People's Council issues "The Declaration of the Establishment of the State of Israel;" five Arab states invade the modern state of Israel the next day.

1967 Six Day War during which Israel captures the West Bank, the Golan, Gaza, and the Sinai Peninsula.

1973 Yom Kippur War.

1979 Israel-Egypt Peace Treaty signed; Israel returns the Sinai Peninsula to Egypt.

1993 Israel signs the Oslo I Accords; the Palestinian Authority is formed to take administrative control of portions of the West Bank and Gaza.

1994 Israel-Jordan Peace Treaty signed.

2005 Israel leaves Gaza entirely, removing all military personnel, as well as all Jews who had been living there.

2005–2014 Hamas launches thousands of missiles from Gaza into Israeli cities.

2006 Hamas wins parliamentary elections in Gaza and the West Bank.

2009 Benjamin Netanyahu gets re-elected as prime minister, ten years after losing an election to hold the office.

2014 The IDF begins the seven-week "Operation Protective Edge," fighting Gaza in an attempt to stop Hamas from firing rockets into Israel.

CHAPTER NOTES

Chapter 1: Meet Ayelet

1. Arnold Dobrin, *A Life for Israel: The Story of Golda Meir* (New York: Dial Press, 1974), p. 57.

Chapter 2: A Walk Down Memory Lane

1. League of Nations, "Mandate for Palestine," August 12, 1922. http://unispal.un.org/UNISPAL.NSF/0/2FCA2C68106F11AB05256BCF007BF3CB

Chapter 3: Jews in Israel

1. Benji Rosen, *Jerusalem Post*, "Israel's Population Reaches More Than 8 Million at Year's End," December 29, 2013. http://www.jpost.com/National-News/Israels-population-reaches-more-than-8-million-at-years-end-336503

2. Ibid.

3. Nurit Yaffe and Dorith Tal, Central Bureau of Statistics Israel, "Immigration to Israel from the Former Soviet Union." http://www.cbs.gov.il/statistical/immigration_e.pdf

4. Clifford J. Levy, *New York Times*, "Israel With a Russian Accent (and Pork)," February 23, 2010. http://www.nytimes.com/2010/02/28/travel/28explorer.html?pagewanted=all&_r=1&

5. Jewish Virtual Library, "Total Immigration from Ethiopia (1948-Present)." https://www.jewishvirtuallibrary.org/jsource/Judaism/ejim.html

6. Moti Bassok, *Haaretz*, "Poll: Fewer than Half of Israelis See Themselves as Secular," September 13, 2010. http://www.haaretz.com/jewish-world/poll-fewer-than-half-of-israelis-see-themselves-as-secular-1.313462

7. Ibid.

8. Ibid.

Chapter 4: Israel's Muslims, Christians, and Druze

1. Elhanan Miller, *Times of Israel*, "Christian Arab MK: We Won't Be Co-Opted Like the Druze," February 27, 2014. http://www.timesofisrael.com/christian-arab-mk-we-wont-be-co-opted-like-the-druze/

2. CNN, WCSC, "Israeli Border Hospital Treating Wounded Syrians," June 26, 2014. http://www.live5news.com/story/25880835/israeli-border-hospital-treating-wounded-syrians

Chapter 5: Six Million Prime Ministers

1. Mayer Fertig, *Jewish Star*, "Review: The Prime Ministers, An Intimate Narrative of Israeli Leadership by Yehuda Avner,"
September 3, 2010. http://www.thejewishstar.com/stories/Review-The-Prime-Ministers-An-Intimate-Narrative-of-Israeli-Leadership-byYehudaAvner,1977

2. Giora Goldberg, *Ben-Gurion against the Knesset* (London: Frank Cass, 2003), p. 144.

3. Israel Ministry of Foreign Affairs, "Basic Law: Human Dignity and Liberty," March 17, 1992. http://www.mfa.gov.il/MFA/MFA-Archive/1992/Pages/Basic%20Law-%20Human%20Dignity%20and%20Liberty-.aspx

4. Asher Schechter, *Haaretz*, "A Short Guide to Israel's Social Protest," July 11, 2012. http://www.haaretz.com/news/national/a-short-guide-to-israel-s-social-protest-1.450369

5. Ibid.

Chapter 6: Israel and the World

1. Barak Ravid, *Haaretz*, "Netanyahu: We Have Consensus on Two-State Solution," July 5, 2009. http://www.haaretz.com/news/netanyahu-we-have-consensus-on-two-state-solution-1.279374

2. Israel Democracy Institute, "The Peace Index—October 2013." http://www.peaceindex.org/files/Peace%20Index%20Data%20-%20October%202013%20-%20Eng.pdf

3. JNS.org, *Algemeiner*, "63% of Israelis Oppose Terrorist Prisoner Release, Poll Says," March 30, 2014. http://www.algemeiner.com/2014/03/30/63-of-israelis-oppose-terrorist-prisoner-release-poll-says/

4. Ephraim Yaar and Tamar Hermann, Israel Democracy Institute, "Peace Index, December 2013." http://en.idi.org.il/media/2943590/Peace_Index_December_2013-Eng.pdf

5. *Jerusalem Post*, "65% of Israelis Say No Danger of New Holocaust," April 3, 2013. http://www.jpost.com/Israel/65-percent-of-Israelis-say-no-danger-of-new-Holocaust-308529

6. Tia Goldenberg, *Times of Israel*, "Chorus of Israeli Voices Renews Calls for Iran Strike," March 21, 2014. http://www.timesofisrael.com/chorus-of-israeli-voices-renews-calls-for-iran-strike/

What You Should Know About Israel

1. Oded Yaron, *Haaretz*, "Israelis Lead World in Social Network Use, U.S. Study Shows," December 22, 2011. http://www.haaretz.com/news/national/israelis-lead-world-in-social-network-use-u-s-study-shows-1.402981

FURTHER READING

Books

Derovan, David. *Israeli Culture in Perspective.* Hockessin, DE: Mitchell Lane Publishers, 2015.

Newberger Speregen, Devra. *Yoni Netanyahu: Commando at Entebbe.* Philadelphia: Jewish Publication Society, 2001.

Schroeter, Daniel J. *Israel: An Illustrated History.* New York: Oxford University Press, 1998.

Sofer, Barbara. *Keeping Israel Safe.* Minneapolis, MN: Lerner Publishing Group, 2008.

On the Internet

My Jewish Learning: "Israel: The Jewish Homeland" http://www.myjewishlearning.com/israel.shtml

Time for Kids Around the World: "Israel" http://www.timeforkids.com/destination/israel

TimeMaps History Atlas: "Middle East History Timeline" http://www.timemaps.com/history/middle-east-1000bc

Works Consulted

Ashkenazi, Eli. "Some 700 Syrians Treated in Israeli Hospitals Since Early 2013." *Haaretz,* January 30, 2014. http://www.haaretz.com/news/national/.premium-1.571622

Axelrod, Alan, and Charles L. Phillips. "Israel-Palestine Liberation Organization Peace Agreements." *Encyclopedia of Historical Treaties and Alliances: From the 1930s to the Present,* vol. 2. New York: Facts On File, Inc., 2006. http://www.fofweb.com/History/MainPrintPage.asp?iPin=treaties00215&DataType=WorldHistory&WinType=Free

Barak, Aharon. "Some Reflections on the Israeli Legal System and Its Judiciary." *Electronic Journal of Comparative Law,* Vol. 6.1, April 2002. http://www.ejcl.org/61/art61-1.html

Bassok, Moti. "Poll: Fewer Than Half of Israelis See Themselves as Secular." *Haaretz,* September 13, 2010. http://www.haaretz.com/jewish-world/poll-fewer-than-half-of-israelis-see-themselves-as-secular-1.313462

BBC News. "Israel Launches Economic Plan for Israeli Arab Towns." March 21, 2010. http://news.bbc.co.uk/2/hi/8576282.stm

Booth, William, and Anne Gearan. "Israelis, Palestinians Begin to Assign Blame for Possible Collapse of Peace Talks." *Washington Post,* April 2, 2014. http://www.washingtonpost.com/world/palestinian-bid-for-stronger-un-ties-throws-peace-talks-into-confusion/2014/04/02/7595734c-ba54-11e3-a397-6debf9e66e65_story.html

Case Bryant, Christa. "Enemies? No, Patients, Say Israeli Doctors Treating Syrians." *Christian Science Monitor,* March 12, 2014. http://www.csmonitor.com/World/Middle-East/Olive-Press/2014/0312/Enemies-No-patients-say-Israeli-doctors-treating-Syrians

Chabad.org. "Shavuos Glass Vase." http://www.chabad.org/kids/article_cdo/aid/364263/jewish/Glass-Vase.htm

Chance, Matthew. "Israel Releases Palestinian Prisoners Amid Protests." CNN.com, October 30, 2013. http://edition.cnn.com/2013/10/29/world/meast/israel-palestinian-prisoner-release/

CNN. "Israeli Border Hospital Treating Wounded Syrians." WCSC, June 26, 2014. http://www.live5news.com/story/25880835/israeli-border-hospital-treating-wounded-syrians

Cohen, Ben. "Christian IDF Recruitment Numbers Affirm Israeli Democracy." *Algemeiner,* November 18, 2013. http://www.algemeiner.com/2013/11/18/christian-idf-recruitment-numbers-affirm-israeli-democracy/

Cruise O'Brien, Conor. *The Siege: The Saga of Israel and Zionism.* New York: Simon & Schuster, 1986.

Deutsche Welle. "Ultra-Orthodox Jews Hold Rally in Jerusalem against Universal Conscription Bill." March 2, 2014. http://www.dw.de/ultra-orthodox-jews-hold-rally-in-jerusalem-against-universal-conscription-bill/a-17468306

Dobrin, Arnold. *A Life for Israel: The Story of Golda Meir.* New York: Dial Press, 1974.

Englander, David, ed. *The Jewish Enigma.* London: Peter Halban Publishers, 1992.

Esensten, Andrew. "Samaritans Make Annual Sacrifice—and Preserve a Way of Life." *Haaretz,* April 23, 2013. http://www.haaretz.com/news/national/samaritans-make-annual-sacrifice-and-preserve-a-way-of-life.premium-1.517378

Fertig, Mayer. "Review: The Prime Ministers, An Intimate Narrative of Israeli Leadership by Yehuda Avner." *Jewish Star,* September 3, 2010. http://www.thejewishstar.com/stories/Review-The-Prime-Ministers-An-Intimate-Narrative-of-Israeli-Leadership-byYehudaAvner,1977

G., Ayelet (eleven-year-old Israeli girl). Interview with the author, April 1, 2014.

Goldberg, Giora. *Ben-Gurion against the Knesset.* London: Frank Cass, 2003.

Goldenberg, Tia. "Chorus of Israeli Voices Renews Calls for Iran Strike." *Times of Israel,* March 21, 2014. http://www.timesofisrael.com/chorus-of-israeli-voices-renews-calls-for-iran-strike/

FURTHER READING

Gorzewski, Andreas. "Hamas Uses Kidnapping as a Strategic Tool." *Deutsche Welle*, July 22, 2014. http://www.dw.de/hamas-uses-kidnapping-as-a-strategic-tool/a-17799249

Halsall, Paul. "Josephus (37–after 93 CE): Galilee, Samaria, and Judea in the First Century CE." *Ancient History Sourcebook*, Fordham University, May 1998. http://www.fordham.edu/halsall/ancient/josephus-wara.asp

Harel, Amos. "Iron Dome Racks Up 90% Success Rate So Far." *Haaretz*, July 9, 2014. http://www.haaretz.com/news/diplomacy-defense/1.604039

Harkov, Lahav. "MK Levy-Abecasis Proposes Lowering Voting Age to 17." *Jerusalem Post*, May 27, 2014. http://www.jpost.com/Diplomacy-and-Politics/MK-Levy-Abecasis-proposes-lowering-voting-age-to-17-354520

Hasson, Nir. "More East Jerusalem Palestinians Seeking Israeli Citizenship, Report Shows." *Haaretz*, April 22, 2013. http://www.haaretz.com/news/diplomacy-defense/more-east-jerusalem-palestinians-seeking-israeli-citizenship-report-shows.premium-1.516906

Ho, Spencer. "Food Prices in Israel 25% Higher than in Europe." *Times of Israel*, January 8, 2014. http://www.timesofisrael.com/food-prices-in-israel-25-higher-than-in-europe/

Israel Democracy Institute. "Majority of Israeli Jews Oppose Withdrawal to '67 Borders with Land Swaps; Large Majority of Israelis Favor Peace Referendum." August 6, 2013. http://en.idi.org.il/about-idi/news-and-updates/majority-of-israeli-jews-oppose-withdrawal-to-67-borders-with-land-swaps-large-majority-of-israelis-favor-peace-referendum/

———. "The Peace Index—October 2013." http://www.peaceindex.org/files/Peace%20Index%20Data%20-%20October%202013%20-%20Eng.pdf

Israel Hayom. "Poll: Israelis Don't Believe Iran Will Stop Nuclear Program." November 25, 2013. http://www.israelhayom.com/site/newsletter_article.php?id=13561

Israel Ministry of Foreign Affairs. "Basic Law: Human Dignity and Liberty." March 17, 1992. http://www.mfa.gov.il/MFA/MFA-Archive/1992/Pages/Basic%20Law-%20Human%20Dignity%20and%20Liberty-.aspx

———. "History: Second Temple Period—Return to Zion." http://www.mfa.gov.il/mfa/aboutisrael/history/pages/history-%20the%20second%20temple.aspx

JCRC of Greater Boston. "Background: Who Are the Ethiopian Jews?" http://www.jcrcboston.org/focus/strength/ethiopian-jewry/background-who-are-the.html

Jerusalem Post. "65% of Israelis Say No Danger of New Holocaust." April 3, 2013. http://www.jpost.com/Israel/65-percent-of-Israelis-say-no-danger-of-new-Holocaust-308529

Jewish Agency for Israel. "The Story of Zionism." http://jafi.org/JewishAgency/English/Jewish+Education/Compelling+Content/Eye+on+Israel/Story_Zionism/Introducing+Zion.htm

Jewish Virtual Library. "Total Immigration from Ethiopia (1948-Present)." https://www.jewishvirtuallibrary.org/jsource/Judaism/ejim.html

JNS.org. "63% of Israelis Oppose Terrorist Prisoner Release, Poll Says." *Algemeiner*, March 30, 2014. http://www.algemeiner.com/2014/03/30/63-of-israelis-oppose-terrorist-prisoner-release-poll-says/

JTA. "Israeli Cabinet Endorses Plan Giving PLO Formal Recognition." September 13, 1993. http://www.jta.org/1993/09/13/archive/israeli-cabinet-endorses-plan-giving-plo-formal-recognition

Keinon, Herb. "Counter-Terrorism Bureau Releases Passover-Season Travel Advisories for 31 Countries." *Jerusalem Post*, April 1, 2014. http://www.jpost.com/National-News/Counter-Terrorism-Bureau-releases-Passover-season-travel-advisories-for-31-countries-347166

League of Nations. "Mandate for Palestine." August 12, 1922. http://unispal.un.org/UNISPAL.NSF/0/2FCA2C68106F11AB05256BCF007BF3CB

Levy, Clifford J. "Israel with a Russian Accent (and Pork)." *New York Times*, February 23, 2010. http://www.nytimes.com/2010/02/28/travel/28explorer.html?pagewanted=all&_r=0

Lewis, Bernard. *The Middle East: A Brief History of the Last 2,000 Years*. New York: Scribner, 1995.

———. *The Shaping of the Modern Middle East*. New York: Oxford University Press, 1994.

Lis, Jonathan. "Israel Raises Electoral Threshold to 3.25 Percent." *Haaretz*, March 12, 2014. http://www.haaretz.com/news/national/1.579289

Mazar, Amihai. *Archaeology of the Land of the Bible: 10,000–586 B.C.E.* New York: Doubleday, 1992.

———. "Archaeology and the Biblical Narrative: The Case of the United Monarchy." *One God—One Cult—One Nation: Archaeological and Biblical Perspectives*, Edited by Reinhard G. Kratz and Hermann Spieckermann. New York: Walter de Gruyter GmbH, 2010.

Melman, Yossi. "In Depth: How Iranian Weapons Reach Hezbollah." *Jerusalem Post*, May 25, 2014. http://www.jpost.com/Defense/In-Depth-How-Iranian-weapons-go-through-Syria-to-Hezbollah-314313

Meron, Ya'akov. "Why Jews Fled the Arab Countries." *Middle East Quarterly*, September 1995. http://www.meforum.org/263/why-jews-fled-the-arab-countries

FURTHER READING

Miller, Elhanan. "Christian Arab MK: We Won't Be Co-Opted Like the Druze." *Times of Israel*, February 27, 2014. http://www.timesofisrael.com/christian-arab-mk-we-wont-be-co-opted-like-the-druze/

Moran, Lee. "'Kill All Jews and Annihilate Israel!' Iran's Ayatollah Lays out Legal and Religious Justification for Attack." *Mail Online*, February 8, 2012. http://www.dailymail.co.uk/news/article-2097252/Kill-Jews-annihilate-Israel-Irans-supreme-leader-lays-legal-religious-justification-attack.html

Norwich, John Julius. *The Middle Sea.* New York: Vintage Books, 2006.

Rabin, Chaim. *A Short History of the Hebrew Language.* Jerusalem: Alpha Press, 1963.

Ravid, Barak. "Netanyahu: We Have Consensus on Two-State Solution." *Haaretz*, July 5, 2009. http://www.haaretz.com/news/netanyahu-we-have-consensus-on-two-state-solution-1.279374

Reuters. "In Pictures: Christians Celebrate Holy Fire in Jerusalem." *Jerusalem Post*, April 19, 2014. http://www.jpost.com/National-News/In-Pictures-Christians-celebrate-Holy-Fire-in-Jerusalem-349916

Richter, Paul. "Iran is Pushing Limits on Nuclear Deal, Former Obama Advisor Warns." *Los Angeles Times*, July 20, 2014. http://www.latimes.com/world/middleeast/la-fg-obama-advisor-iran-nuclear-20140720-story.html

Rivka, Sara. "Sukkah Lanterns from Recycled Soda Bottles. . . . In Progress." *Creative Jewish Mom*, September 13, 2013. http://www.creativejewishmom.com/2013/09/sukkah-lanterns-from-recycled-soda-bottles.html

Robertson, Nic. "A Modern Day Wonder in the Sea of Galilee, Israel's Hotspot for Migratory Birds." CNN, April 9, 2014. http://www.cnn.com/2014/04/09/travel/israel-bird-migrations-sea-galilee/

Rolef, Susan Hattis. "The Competition and Its Results, Mid-1956 to Mid-1958." *The Knesset Building in Giv'at Ram—Planning and Construction.* July 2000. https://www.knesset.gov.il/building/architecture/eng/art1_contest_eng.htm

Rosen, Benji. "Israel's Population Reaches More Than 8 Million at Year's End." *Jerusalem Post*, December 29, 2013. http://www.jpost.com/National-News/Israels-population-reaches-more-than-8-million-at-years-end-336503

Rudoren, Jodi, and Isabel Kershner. "Israel's Pairing Prisoner Release and Settlements Angers Many." *New York Times*, December 30, 2013. http://www.nytimes.com/2013/12/31/world/middleeast/israel-prisoner-release-settlements.html?pagewanted=1&_r=0

Schechter, Asher. "A Short Guide to Israel's Social Protest." *Haaretz*, July 11, 2012. http://www.haaretz.com/news/national/a-short-guide-to-israel-s-social-protest-1.450369

Schwartz, Adi. "Israel's Christian Awakening." *Wall Street Journal*, December 27, 2013. http://online.wsj.com/news/articles/SB10001424052702303849604579278722657163880

State of Israel. "The Knesset in the Government System." https://www.knesset.gov.il/description/eng/eng_mimshal0.htm

Times of Israel. "Netanyahu Indicates He Wants Fourth Term as PM." April 17, 2013. http://www.timesofisrael.com/netanyahu-indicates-he-wants-fourth-term-as-pm/

Tobianah, Vicky. "Pianist Explores Hatikvah's Origins." *Canadian Jewish News*, April 13, 2012. http://www.cjnews.com/arts/pianist-explores-hatikvah's-origins

Urquart, Conal, Ian Black, and Mark Tran. "Hamas Takes Control of Gaza." *Guardian*, June 15, 2007. http://www.theguardian.com/world/2007/jun/15/israel4

Witte, Griff, and Ruth Eglash. "Iron Dome, Israel's Antimissile System, Changes Calculus of Fight with Hamas." *Washington Post*, July 17, 2014. http://www.washingtonpost.com/world/middle_east/israel-shoots-down-hamas-drone/2014/07/14/991c46da-0b47-11e4-b8e5-d0de80767fc2_story.html

Yaar, Ephraim, and Tamar Hermann. "Peace Index, December 2013." Israel Democracy Institute, Tel Aviv University. http://en.idi.org.il/media/2943590/Peace_Index_December_2013-Eng.pdf

———. "Peace Index November 2013." Israel Democracy Institute, Tel Aviv University. http://en.idi.org.il/media/2907334/Peace%20Index%20November%202013%20-%20Eng.pdf

Yaffe, Nurit, and Dorith Tal. "Immigration to Israel from the Former Soviet Union." Central Bureau of Statistics Israel. http://www.cbs.gov.il/statistical/immigration_e.pdf

Yaron, Oded. "Israelis Lead World in Social Network Use, U.S. Study Shows." *Haaretz*, December 22, 2011. http://www.haaretz.com/news/national/israelis-lead-world-in-social-network-use-u-s-study-shows-1.402981

GLOSSARY

annex (uh-NEKS, or AN-eks)—To take control of an area of land and make it part of a country or state.

anti-Semitism (an-tee-SEM-i-tiz-uhm)—Discrimination against or hatred of Jews.

atheist (EY-thee-ist)—A person who doesn't believe in the existence of God or gods.

civil marriage—A marriage conducted by a government authority, like a judge, instead of religious authority, like a rabbi.

consensus (kuhn-SEN-suhs)—Majority opinion or general agreement.

denomination (dih-nom-uh-NEY-shuhn)—A subgroup within the same religion, usually separated by differences in religious belief or ritual; examples are Protestant and Catholic Christians, or Sunni and Shiite Muslims.

Diaspora (dahy-AS-per-uh)—The term used to describe Jews living outside of Israel; it refers to the Jewish community being dispersed throughout the world after losing their homeland.

domestic (duh-MES-tik)—Referring to issues and politics within a single country.

exile (EG-zahyl)—To be forced away from one's native country and not allowed to return.

Holy Temple—A massive religious and ceremonial building built in Jerusalem on Judaism's most holy site; the First Holy Temple was believed to house the Ten Commandments; it survived four hundred years before being destroyed in 586 BCE by the Babylonians; a Second Holy Temple was built later, but was destroyed by the Romans in 70 CE.

leavened (LEV-uhnd)—Refers to bread that has risen.

Mandatory Palestine (MAN-duh-tawr-ee PAL-uh-stahyn)—Refers to an area of land in the Middle East put under British control in 1922 through a mandate from the League of Nations. The mandate formally ended in 1948. Today, that land includes Israel, Gaza, and the West Bank.

mosque (MOSK)—A Muslim place of worship.

nomadic (noh-MAD-ik)—Refers to a tribe which has no fixed home, but moves along a large expanse of land with all their belongings to find food, water, and open pasture to graze their animals.

nuclear weapon (NOO-klee-er)—A device which splits or combines the nuclei of atoms to release energy, resulting in a highly destructive explosion.

orthopedic shoes (awr-thuh-PEE-dik)—Shoes that are designed to provide comfort and support for people with foot or ankle disorders.

prophet (PROF-it)—A person who speaks to other people on behalf of God.

prosthetics (pros-THET-iks)—Artificial body parts.

rabbi (RAB-ahy)—A Jewish religious leader who is ordained to perform Jewish rituals and make decisions regarding Jewish law.

rabbinic Judaism (ruh-BIN-ik JOO-dee-iz-uhm)—Dominant form of Judaism today; dating to the sixth century when the Talmud set down the oral law and became the authoritative source for understanding religious texts.

revolt (ri-VOHLT)—To rebel against government authority, usually in a violent way.

secular (SEK-yuh-ler)—Not connected to a religion.

socialism (SOH-shuh-liz-uhm)—An economic theory based on common ownership of property and a person's labor, usually controlled through government.

Soviet Union (SOH-vee-et)—Short name for the Union of Soviet Socialist Republics, this was a large communist country that existed from 1922 to 1991, comprised of Russia and many smaller states bordering Russia.

Spanish Inquisition (in-kwuh-ZISH-uhn)—A Catholic court set up in Spain in the fifteenth century to find Jews and Muslims who had converted to Catholicism but were still secretly practicing Judaism or Islam. At this time, Jews and Muslims had been required to convert to Catholicism or be expelled from the country. Those who were found guilty of practicing a religion other than Catholicism were killed or imprisoned.

suicide bombing—An attack in which the attacker bombs a location where he or she is present, thus killing him or herself in addition to those in the area; this often done by the bomber wearing a belt wired with explosives.

synagogue (SIN-uh-gog)—A Jewish house of worship.

terrorism (TER-uh-riz-uhm)—Violence which is used to intimidate people and governments into giving into specific political demands.

Zionism (ZAHY-uh-niz-uhm)—The philosophy that Jews should have an independent Jewish country in their native homeland.

INDEX

About the Author

Elisa Silverman is a freelance writer who's written a number of books [on] Israel for Mitchell Lane Publishers. Originally from Chicago, Elisa h[as] lived in Jerusalem, Israel, for over a decade. She's also lived in Spain a[nd] Japan, and traveled widely throughout the world.

In addition to educational materials, she creates business-to-busine[ss] content, and writes on legal and travel topics. Elisa was graduated fr[om] Brandeis University with a bachelor's degree in philosophy, and holds [a] law degree from Emory University School of Law. While traveling is o[ne] of Elisa's favorite activities, she also enjoys yoga, the arts, and rema[ins] very committed to Chicago's sports teams. You can follow Elisa on Twit[ter] @ElisaKapha.

ISRAEL